# 13 Artists
## Children Should Know

Angela Wenzel

PRESTEL

Munich · London · New York

# Contents

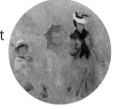

**13** great artists are introduced in this book, which tells you about where and when they lived and what ideas they tried to put across in their paintings. Of course it also shows you some of their most famous pictures. You can answer the quiz questions and find ideas for your own works of art. A timeline gives you an idea of important events which took place during each artist's lifetime. And at the back of the book you'll find an explanation of some of the special words used which are marked in the text with a star*.

Have fun reading and painting your own pictures!

**Mona Lisa, 1503–1506**
Musée du Louvre, Paris

The *Mona Lisa* is probably the most famous painting in the world. Today you can only admire it through bullet-proof glass. The lady is thought to have been the wife of a merchant, Francesco del Giocondo, who came from Florence; that is why the *Mona Lisa* is also known by the Italian name *La Gioconda*. Leonardo painted her with a delicate, glowing complexion and a mysterious smile. It doesn't matter which side you approach the painting from—she always looks as if she is watching you. The landscape in the background disappears into a fine veil of mist. The picture belonged to the King of France, Francis I. Leonardo spent the final years of his life in the king's castle in Cloux.

# Leonardo da Vinci— Madonnas and Flying Machines

Leonardo da Vinci was what is called a "universal genius"— a brilliant all-rounder: a painter, sculptor, architect, engineer, and scientist all rolled into one.

**Born:**
April 15, 1452 in the village of Anchiano near Vinci, Italy
**Died:**
May 2, 1519 in Cloux, France
**Lived in:**
Florence, Milan, Rome, Cloux
**Era:**
Renaissance*

We are told that Leonardo was handsome and strong, and a talented and clever speaker. His thirst for knowledge was unquenchable. In that respect he was typical of the age in which he lived, the Renaissance*. At that time, people had started to look into the importance of nature and were influenced by the Ancient Greeks and Romans.

Mathematics and geometry, physics, engineering, anatomy, geology, botany and geography, music, sculpture, painting— Leonardo was an expert in all subjects. He invented weapons and machines for the Duke of Milan. He carried out detailed experiments to investigate the movement of water. He was even interested in the idea of flying.

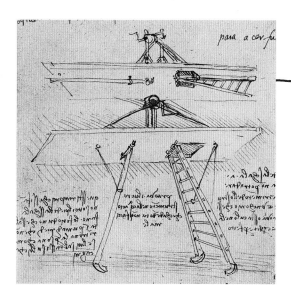

**Aircraft with ladders as landing gear**
MS. D. Institut de France, Paris

Leonardo made detailed drawings of his discoveries and inventions. However, it was not only as a scientist but also as an artist that he searched for new ideas. For him, painting was the most important of all sciences.

Leonardo wrote down everything he had discovered in his notebooks—in mirror writing. He was left-handed, and for him it was faster to write that way.
Can you write your name in mirror writing?

Leonardo was famous even during his lifetime. Monasteries and churches asked him to paint them scenes from the Bible. Princes, the King of France, and the Pope competed for his attention. Leonardo always had big plans, but he did not always manage to complete them—much to the annoyance of his customers.

**The Last Supper,
1495–97**
Monastery of Santa Maria delle Grazie, Milan

On the evening before he was arrested, Jesus divided the bread and wine among his twelve disciples at the Last Supper. Leonardo shows him in the moment when he tells them that one of them will betray him. The sudden movements show the disciples' surprise. Only Christ himself remains calm. Judas, the traitor, is quite easy to pick out. Can you find him? He is holding a purse of money in his hand.

Leonardo painted this picture on the wall in the refectory of the Dominican Monastery of Santa Maria delle Grazie in Milan. He used a technique which he had invented himself but the painting soon began to peel off the wall and marks started to appear on the picture. It has had to be restored* several times already. Even so, the overall composition is still clearly visible.

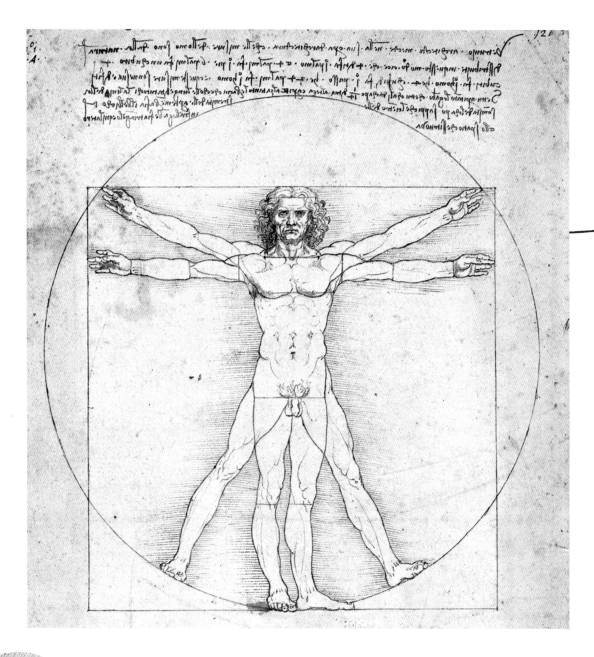

**Vitruvian Man,
c. 1490**
Galleria dell'Accademia,
Venice

Leonardo examined dead
bodies in order to find
out about the structure
of the skeleton and
muscles and the position
of the various organs.
He was convinced that a
painter needed to know
about the anatomy* of
the body in order to be
able to paint people pro-
perly.

**Tips**
The Museo Leonardiano
in Vinci is full of information about Leonard's
scientific research and
shows models of his
flying machines and
apparatus (www.leonet.
it/communi/vincimus).
And in Anchiano you can
visit the house in which
Leonardo was born.

**Further reading**
*Who can crack the
Leonardo da Vinci Code?*
by Thomas Brezina
(in Prestel's Museum of
Adventures series)

**Studies of Cats and Dragons**
Royal Collection,
Windsor Castle

Leonardo seems to have been
fascinated by dragons. As a boy
he scared other children with a
toy dragon he had made, and
as an old man he stuck wings,
horns and a beard on a lizard
he had tamed—and used it to
frighten his friends.

# Jan Vermeer—The Secret of His Glowing Colors

**Born:**
October 31, 1632 in Delft, The Netherlands
**Died:** December 15, 1675 in Delft
**Lived in:** Delft
**Children:** Eleven, two of whom died in childhood
**Era:** Baroque*
**Unusual fact:** Vermeer also ran a tavern and worked as an art dealer

Jan Vermeer liked to paint at home more than anywhere else. That is where he had his studio, and where he found ideas for his work.

The Dutch painter's pictures often show scenes of domestic life during his times. We call paintings of this kind "genre paintings". They were very popular during the 17th century in the Netherlands. Vermeer chose colors that look particularly rich.

Nobody could paint such a deep and intense blue, or such a bright red and brilliant yellow, as he did. Vermeer's favorite shade of blue is even known as "Vermeer blue" today. In those days, artists used to mix their own colors from pigments* according to their own recipes. Vermeer's colors glow from within. That is partly because of his special painting technique: He painted several thin layers of color on top of each other. The bottom layers of paint then shine through the ones put on top.

**The Art of Painting, c. 1666/67**
Kunsthistorisches Museum, Vienna

This picture gives us a glimpse of his artist's studio. He is just painting the laurel garland that his model is wearing. Vermeer left nothing to chance. Each object was carefully selected, and the arrangement and choice of colors carefully thought out.

### The Girl with a Pearl Earring, c. 1665
Mauritshuis, The Hague

The girl is looking at us and seems to want to tell us something. What do you think it might be? No one knows who she is. Was it perhaps one of Vermeer's daughters? The girl with the pearl earring has roused the imagination of many people. A novel about her became a best-seller that was then made into a film in 2003. The made-up story tells us that the girl was a servant In the Vermeer household.

**Quiz**
Do you know which stone was used in the olden days to produce a precious blue paint?
(Answer on p. 46)

✳ 1826 Joseph Niéphore Niépce takes the first photograph — 1870 Revolution in Paris ✳

Claude Monet 1840–1926
Mary Cassatt 1844–1926
Henri Rousseau 1844–1910

1870–1871 Franco-Prussian War

1820    1825    1830    1835    1840    1845    1850    1855    1860    1865    1870    187

**Poppy Field near Argenteuil, 1873**
Musée d'Orsay, Paris

Complementary colors like red and green, blue and orange, and yellow and purple, glow even more brilliantly when used together. Monet used this to his advantage to paint especially radiant pictures. Here we see red and green together. The red seems even brighter when surrounded by green. The people going for a walk are quite hard to see in the middle of the poppy field. How many are there?

**Rouen Cathedral, 1892**
Private collection

Monet painted several pictures of the cathedral in Rouen at various times of day. It looks a different color each time. The sharp contours and hard surface of the stone are broken up into colored dots of light.

**Rouen Cathedral, 1892**
Museum of Fine Arts, Boston

# Claude Monet—Light and Colors

Claude Monet preferred to paint outside. That meant that he could always study the countryside, people, and things in the constantly changing light.

Monet was not interested in what color things really were or the material they were made of. He wanted to record the fleeting impression of a particular moment.

Have you ever noticed the way colors change according to the light: That a house, for instance, looks quite different in the cool light of dawn than it does in the warm evening light of the setting sun? Or how different it looks on a gray day compared to bright sunlight? It was these impressions that Monet wanted to paint: The sparkle of light; the interplay between sun and shadow; dancing colors.

**Born:** November 14, 1840 in Paris
**Died:** December 5, 1926 in Giverny
**Lived in:**
Le Havre, Paris, Etretat, Giverny
**Children:**
Two children of his own with his first wife Camille (Jean, Michel) and six from the first marriage of his second wife, Alice
**Hobby:** Gardening
**Painting style:**
Impressionism*

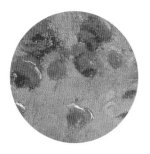

**Arrival of the Normandy Train, Gare Saint-Lazare, 1877**
The Art Institute of Chicago

In Monet's time the railroad and automobiles were new inventions, and they fascinated him. In this picture he has concentrated especially on the steam in the station.

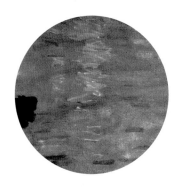

When he was still young, Monet became one of the founders of Impressionism*. Many years were to pass, however, before the general public started to like Impressionist painting—years during which Monet and his family lived in poverty and had to put up with a great deal of mockery from the art critics. Later, however, he emerged as one of the most famous artists in Paris and became extremely rich.

**Impression: Sunrise, 1872**
Musée Marmottan, Paris

This is one of Monet's most famous pictures. It shows the harbor at Le Havre. What the artist found most important was to capture the reflections of the sunlight and to portray the morning mist. The short brushstrokes make the light seem to flicker. It was after the title of this painting, "Impression," that Monet and his painter friends came to be known as Impressionists*. At first the word was not meant nicely, but today Impressionism refers to a movement in art.

**Suggestions for further reading**
*Claude Monet: The Magician of Color* by Stephen Koja (in Prestel's Adventures in Art series); *Linnea in Monet's Garden* by Cristina Bjork, Lena Anderson, and Joan Sandin

In 1890 Monet bought a house in the village of Giverny near Paris where he lived with his family. It had a large garden which Monet planted with lots of flowers and blossoming shrubs in bright color combinations. Most important of all, he had a humongous pond dug, planted it with water lilies, and had a Japanese-style bridge built across it. That meant that he could watch the wonderful play of color and light which he needed for his paintings just by stepping outside his front door. Even when he was old and almost blind, Monet sat outdoors and painted impressions of his garden.

**Water Lilies, 1916–19**
Musée Marmottan, Paris

Some of Monet's water lily paintings are so large that they give us the impression that we could dive right into the picture.

After Monet's death his step-daughter Blanche continued to look after the garden. Later it became more and more neglected, but was then carefully restored during the 1970s. Today you can admire Monet's house and garden with the water-lily pond in all its glory in the village of Giverny, about 70 km (44 miles) north of Paris.

1871 Revolution in Paris ✾

Henri Rousseau 1844–1910
Claude Monet 1840–1926
Mary Cassatt 1844–1926

1870–1871 Franco-Prussian War

| 1820 | 1825 | 1830 | 1835 | 1840 | 1845 | 1850 | 1855 | 1860 | 1865 | 1870 | 1875 |

**Born:**
May 21, 1844 in Laval, Brittany, France
**Died:**
September 2, 1910 in Paris
**Lived in:** Paris
**Children:**
Nine, of whom only two reached adulthood: Julia and Henri-Anatole
**Profession:**
Customs officer
**Painting style:**
Naïve

# Henri Rousseau— The "Painting Customs Officer"

Henri Rousseau has gone down in art history as "le Douanier," the "Customs Officer." He earned his living working for the customs department in Paris and painted in his spare time.

At the age of 49 he retired because he wanted to spend all his time painting. He never attended art college or an academy. In order to learn how to compose a picture he copied paintings by the Old Masters in museums. And more than anything else, he liked visiting the Botanical Gardens in Paris, where he lived. He studied the tropical plants and dreamed of the jungle and faraway lands.

**The Sleeping Gypsy, 1897**
Museum of Modern Art, New York

Are the lion and the woman in the moonlight just an apparition or is the woman perhaps dreaming of the lion?

14

**The Dream, 1910**
Museum of Modern Art, New York

Rousseau's far-off worlds are both magical and mysterious—right down to the animals hidden behind the leaves in the jungle. What creatures can you find in this picture?

To make himself sound more interesting Rousseau made up the story that he was one of only a handful of soldiers who had returned unharmed from a French army expedition to Mexico. In fact, however, the only faraway countries he ever went to were in his dreams!

During his lifetime Rousseau had only one solo exhibition. Many people thought he was a just another hobby painter. Others, however, considered him as a great artist. They were impressed by the mysterious, fairy-tale moods in his paintings, and by his use of unusual colors and the way he saw the world in general. Soon after Rousseau's death collectors and museums competed to buy his works, which can be seen today in the best museums in the world.

**Paint the jungle the way you think it looks!**

**Further reading**
*Henri Rousseau's Jungle Book* by Doris Kutschbach; *Henri Rousseau: A Jungle Expedition* by Susanne Pfleger (both in Prestel's Adventures in Art series)

15

1865 American President Abraham Lincoln is assassinated
Mary Cassatt 1844–1926
Claude Monet 1840–1926
Henri Rousseau 1844–1910
1869 The railroad is built across the United States from East to West

1820    1825    1830    1835    1840    1845    1850    1855    1860    1865    1870    1875

**Born:**
May 22 1844
in Pittsburgh,
Pennsylvania, USA
**Died:** June 14, 1926
in Le Mesnil-Théribus,
Oise, France
**Lived in:**
United States and
France
**Children:** none
**Painting style:**
Impressionism*

# Mary Cassatt— An American Woman in Paris

Mary Cassatt was an unusual woman: She managed to become famous as an artist. So you think that's not so special? In the nineteenth century it certainly was!

In those days it was not at all usual for women to study and become artists. At art academies* they were not even allowed to take part in the nude drawing classes*. But Mary insisted on having her own way. And she then even became successful in Paris as an American artist!

**Little Girl in a Blue Armchair, 1878**
National Gallery of Art, Washington

Take a seat! Mary Cassatt obviously enjoyed painting the blue flowered sofa and chairs with rapid brush-strokes. The child and the dog both look as if they are comfortable in the big cushy armchairs. Or do you think they look bored?

Paris in those days was the art capital of the world. It was there that artists developed new ideas which then spread throughout Europe and the United States. From the 1870s it was the Impressionists* who attracted all the attention. Mary Cassatt joined them and some—like the painter Edgar Degas—became close friends.

Mary Cassatt mostly painted women, and especially liked to paint mothers with their children. And yet she had no family of her own and never married.

**The Boating Party,
c. 1893/94**
National Gallery of Art,
Washington

Here, it really is as if you are sitting in the boat too! The artist has moved in really close to her choice of subject in this picture. Other Impressionists also zoomed in on the scene to make their paintings look as lively as possible.

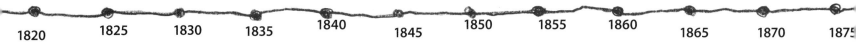

**Self-Portrait with Bandaged Ear, 1889**
Courtauld Institute Galleries, London

Following a violent argument with his artist friend Paul Gauguin, van Gogh was so worked up that he cut off part of his left ear and painted this *Self-Portrait with Bandaged Ear.*

**Quiz**
Why is the bandage in van Gogh's self-portrait on the right?
(Answer on p. 46)

18

# Vincent van Gogh— The Power of Color

Vincent van Gogh never tired of looking at colors. He used colors to express his feelings.

**Born:**
March 30 1853 in Groot-Zundert, Brabant, The Netherlands
**Died:** July 29, 1890
**Lived in:** Paris, London, The Hague, Antwerp, and Arles amongst other places
**Children:** none
**Painting style:**
Late Impressionism*
**Importance:**
The forerunner of Expressionism*

His moods often got the better of him. Sometimes he was very depressed and in despair, and othertimes he was full of joy and hope. Van Gogh did not paint things exactly as they really looked. He exaggerated the colors or even changed them. In his pictures we can see the powerful brush-strokes very clearly. His pictures often tell us about his feelings.

Unfortunately no one wanted to buy his paintings back then. For that reason his brother Theo, who was an art dealer in Paris, always had to support him. During his lifetime van Gogh was best known by young artists. Only after his death did he become really famous. Today van Gogh's paintings are among the most expensive in the world.

**Père Tanguy, 1887**
Musée Rodin, Paris

Père (Father) Tanguy ran a paint store in Paris. Van Gogh painted his friend sitting in front of a wall covered with pictures by Japanese artists. These were very popular at the time, and they provided many artists with lots of new ideas for their own paintings. Van Gogh was also fascinated by them.

**The Bedroom, 1888**
Van Gogh Museum,
Amsterdam

Is your bedroom as bright and colorful as this one? Van Gogh painted his bedroom as yellow as the sun in the South of France and with strong colors. For the picture he chose various complementary colors*. They make the picture glow and at the same time give it a sense of balance. How many complementary pairs of colors can you find?

One day Vincent van Gogh set off for the South of France. He wanted to live and work in peace in a place where the light makes the colors glow. He rented a yellow house in the town of Arles.

Van Gogh planned to make his dream come true and lead the life of an artist. But he also wanted to live and work together with other artists. His painter friend Paul Gauguin accepted his invitation, but the two of them could not get on with each other living at such close quarters. Gauguin only stayed with van Gogh for two months.

Van Gogh then spent a long time in a psychiatric clinic and received medical treatment. He was incurably mentally ill, and in 1890 he committed suicide.

**Sunflowers, 1888**
Neue Pinakothek,
Munich

Van Gogh was looking
forward to Gauguin's arrival in Arles and excitedly
prepared everything
for his friend's stay. He
painted pictures to dec-
orate the guest bedroom.
It looks as if the sun
itself is shining out of
this picture! The cold tur-
quoise in the background
increases the effect of
the warm yellow tones.
Sunflowers were van
Gogh's favorite flowers.
He painted four pictures
of sunflowers in rapid
succession, and another
three the following year.

**Tip**
The Van Gogh Museum in
Amsterdam
(www.vangoghmuseum.
nl) and the Kröller-Müller
Museum (www.kmm.nl) in
Otterlo (The Netherlands)
own the largest collections
of Van Gogh paintings in
the world.

**Further reading**
*Visiting Vincent van Gogh*
by Caroline Breunesse
(in Prestel's Adventures
in Art series); *Who Can
Save Vincent's Hidden
Treasure* by Thomas Brezina
(Museum of Adventures
series)

Do you have a favorite flower? Paint a picture of it in real bright colors!

1850   1855   1860   1865   1870   1875   1880   1885   1890   1895   1900   190

**Born:**
December 31, 1869 in
Le Cateau-Cambrésis,
Picardy, France
**Died:**
November 3, 1954 in
Cimiez near Nice
**Lived in:**
Paris, Issy-les-
Moulineaux, Nice,
Cimiez
**Children:**
Marguérite, Jean,
Pierre
**Painting style:**
Fauvism*
**Special skills**
Cutting silhouettes

# Henri Matisse— The Painter with a Love of Life

Henri Matisse's pictures are a colorful feast for the eyes. The wild colors he put side by side gleam on their own.

At first, other painters at the time found Matisse's brilliant colors too bright, so they called him and his friends who painted in the same way "Fauves"—"The Wild Ones."

**Pierrot's Funeral, 1943/44**

This picture is one of an entire series of colorful cut-outs which Matisse created for his book *Jazz*.

Matisse thought that pictures should be like an armchair in which you can relax and recover from the daily grind. Best of all he liked painting beautiful women. They acted as models for him in his studio, where he both lived and worked. He had decorated the rooms with luxuriant plants, bouquets of flowers, and unusually patterned fabrics.

**The Dance, 1909/10**
The State Hermitage
Museum, St. Petersburg

For his villa in Moscow,
the wealthy art-lover and
collector Sergei Shchukin
asked Matisse to paint
three large paintings for
him. *The Dance* is one of
them. The joy of dancing
and the sweeping motion
are shown in the strong
color contrasts and the
dynamic movement of
the figures.

He was excellent at drawing, but during the last years of his life he developed another special technique: He "drew with scissors," as he called it. To do so his assistants painted paper the color he wanted, and then Matisse would cut out shapes—figures, plants, sea creatures—freehand, without drawing the shapes first. He would sometimes use them to make huge pictures which were a real celebration of line and color.

How about trying to cut out a figure yourself—for example a starfish or a dancer? Take a piece of colored paper (drawing paper or paper which you have already painted all over in your favorite color). You will end up with two copies of your cut-out, one in color and one as a negative (the hole left after cutting out the shape), surrounded by the colored paper. You can then fix them both to a larger sheet.

**Tip**
In Nice, where Matisse
lived for a long time,
there is a museum to his
life and works (www.
musee-matisse-nice.org).

**Further reading**
*Cut-out Fun With Matisse*
by Max and Nina Hollein
(in Prestel's Adventures in
Art series)

**The Twittering Machine, 1922, 151**

Museum of Modern Art, New York

Has somebody just turned the handle on the right? The "Twittering Machine" is going at full speed. The wavy line which the bird-like creatures are sitting on is spinning round and round. Half animal, half machine, they are twittering away as loudly as they can with their feathers flowing! The second twitterer from the right has been singing so energetically that its neck has twisted into a spiral. It looks a bit like a trill in music notation. Which of the bird-like creatures has the highest voice, do you think?

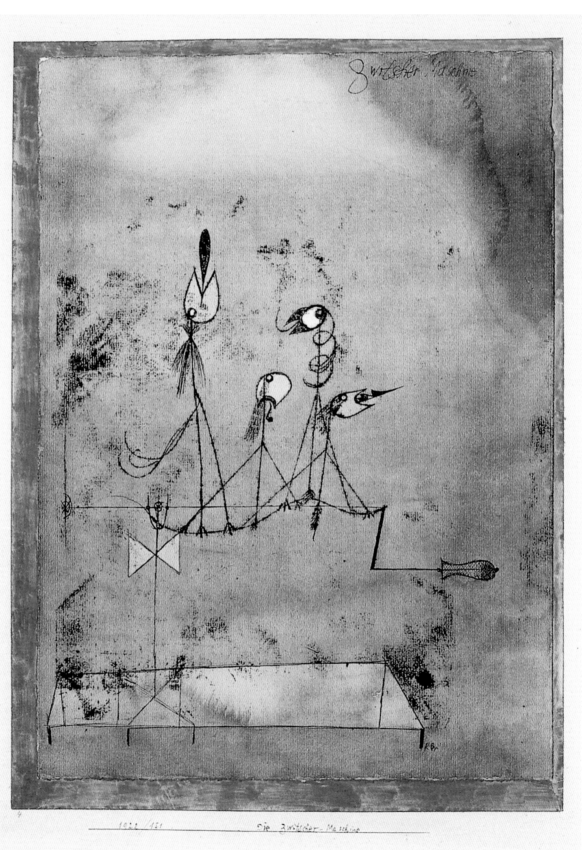

1921 Klee takes up teaching position at the Bauhaus

1933 Adolf Hitler becomes Chancellor of the German Reich. Klee's art is banned. He moves to Bern, Switzerland

1931 Klee moves to the Academy of Art in Düsseldorf

1920    1925    1930    1935    1940    1945    1950    1955    1960    1965    1970    1975

# Paul Klee—Not a Day Without a Line

In the beginning was the dot. Paul Klee always said that if you set a dot in motion it would become a line. And he couldn't imagine a day without a line—in other words, a day without drawing.

Paul Klee tried out various unusual ways of painting and printing. For example, he painted on fabric and plaster or he made oil tracings like the one in *The Twittering Machine* on the opposite page. To do so he colored one side of a sheet of paper black. Then he laid the paper with the black side down on top of a second sheet of paper and drew on the back of the first sheet. All the lines then pressed through in black onto the second sheet, together with a few black marks.

Try to make an oil tracing yourself! Paul Klee used oil paints, but you can use water-soluble acrylic paint instead.

Motif from Hammamet, 1914, 48
Basel, Kupferstichkabinett

**Born:**
December 18, 1879 in Münchenbuchsee, near Bern, Switzerland

**Died:**
December 29, 1940 in Locarno-Muralto, Switzerland

**Lived in:**
Bern, Munich, Weimar, Dessau, Düsseldorf

**Child:** Felix Paul

In April 1914 Paul Klee and his artist friends August Macke and Louis Moilliet traveled to Tunis for two weeks to paint. It was there that Klee produced this watercolor*. This journey to north Africa was very important for Klee's development as an artist and has gone down in art history.

**Landscape with Yellow Birds, 1923, 32**
Private collection,
Switzerland

A mysterious wood: The colors glow strangely out of the darkness. Here, too, Paul Klee used a special technique. He didn't put watercolor on a white background as normal, but used a dark background instead which shines through the other colors.

**Further reading**
*Dreaming Pictures: Paul Klee* by Jürgen von Schemm; *Paul Klee: Animal Tricks* by Christian Rümelin (both in Prestel's Adventures in Art series)

**Painting for young fans**
Big art for little hands: *Paul Klee Coloring Book* (also available from Prestel)

As a young man, Paul Klee could not decide for a long time whether he would rather become a poet, a painter or even a musician. He was an excellent violinist and Lily, his wife, was a pianist. He decided to become an artist, but in his pictures we often find references to notes and music.

The titles of Klee's pictures often sound like the lines of a poem. He decided what to call them while he was still working on them. Klee never copied anything, nor does he tell us a story which has a beginning and an end. His pictures grow out of the colors and lines, just as plants grow in nature.

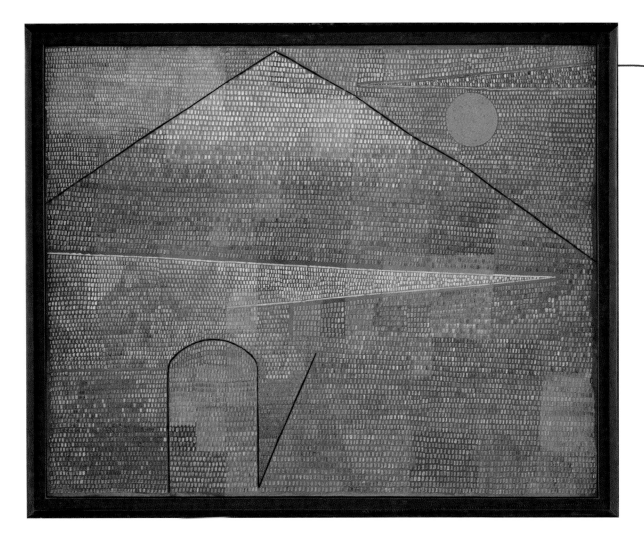

In 1931 Klee became a professor at the Academy of Art* in Düsseldorf. During this time he tried out a new painting technique: Brushstroke by brushstroke, he dabbed blobs of paint in rows against a colored background. This picture shimmers like a mosaic. The orange and yellow shades glow warmly set off against the colder blues and purples. The title refers to Parnassus, a mountain in Greece. The ancient Greeks believed that it was the home of Apollo, the god of poetry and music, and of the Muses.

As a teacher at the Bauhaus* and the Academy of Art* in Düsseldorf, Klee was able to pass on his ideas about art to many students. However, in 1933, when the National Socialists (the Nazis) came to power, Klee's art was banned. He fled to Switzerland, to Bern, where he had grown up—his father was German and his mother Swiss.

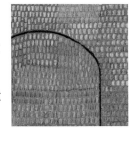

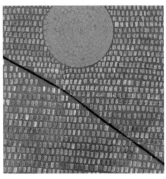

**Tip**
In Bern, Klee's home town, there is a museum called the Paul-Klee-Zentrum (www.zpk.org) which houses a lot of his artworks. On the website under the heading "Kindermuseum Creaviva"—which is all in English too—you can take part in a fun online quiz or go on a journey of discovery in Paul Klee's world of signs and symbols. And in the same children's section you can find a lot of inspiration to paint and experiment yourself.

1911 The artists' group "Der Blaue Reiter" (The Blue Rider) is formed

Franz Marc 1880–1916

Paul Klee 1879–1940

Henri Matisse 1869–1954

1914 -19

1860    1865    1870    1875    1880    1885    1890    1895    1900    1905    1910    1915

**Blue Horse, 1911**
Lenbachhaus, Munich

The color of the horse is meant to show us that it is nearer to the sky than to the ground. Franz Marc thought that animals were closer to Heaven and to Paradise than people. The blue horse looks as if it's thinking about something—what could that be?

# Franz Marc— The Painter of Animals

Franz Marc became famous for his pictures of blue horses, yellow cows, and red cats.

He liked animals better than people as he had often been disappointed by the unreasonableness of many people. He believed that animals were cleverer than we are. They don't try to be better than nature or even destroy it. They adapt to nature and form a part of it. In Marc's opinion, only animals were worthy of living in Paradise. He believed that they might even be able to help us to find it again.

**Born:**
February 8, 1880 in Munich
**Died:**
March 4, 1916 in France during the First World War
**Lived in:**
Upper Bavaria, Germany (Munich, Ried near Kochel)
**Children:** none
**Painting style:**
Expressionism*
**Favorite color:** Blue
**Favorite animal:** Horse
**Special fact:**
One of the founders of the artists' group "Der Blaue Reiter"

Cows—Red, Green, Yellow, 1912
Lenbachhaus Munich

All the shapes in this picture are soft and round; that is why it looks so harmonious and cheerful.

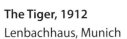

Franz Marc painted animals differently from other artists before him. He didn't want simply to copy them and was not interested in the color of their fur or whether it felt soft. Marc wanted to be part of those animals, so to speak, and see the world as they saw it. He believed that animals had a soul. And that's why he didn't paint them in their natural colors.

**The Tiger, 1912**
Lenbachhaus, Munich

Tiger, tiger, burning bright! What has the predator spotted? When used next to black, yellow stands out like a warning sign. And the zig-zag shapes also mean: Watch out! The tiger is about to pounce!

In nature there are no blue horses and no yellow cows. Franz Marc used these powerful, brilliant colors to express the character and individual qualities of the animals, because for him, the different colors had specific meanings. Yellow was the color of gentleness. He considered red to be a down-to-earth, feminine color. And blue was the color of the spiritual.

**Quiz**
What was the name of the famous group of artists which Franz Marc founded together with his friend Wassily Kandinsky?
(Answer on p. 46)

**Fighting Shapes, 1914**
Pinakothek der Moderne, Munich

During the course of time, the colors Franz Marc used became stronger and the shapes less natural. Eventually the animals disappeared almost entirely. You have to look very hard to work out what these shapes could be. Which animals do you think might be fighting with each other here?

**Tip**
Many of Franz Marc's famous animal pictures can be seen in the Lenbachhaus in Munich. In Kochel, in Upper Bavaria, there is a museum dedicated to the artist and his work (www.franz-marc-museum.de).

That was why the artists' group which he founded in 1911 with Wassily Kandinsky and other artist friends decided on the name "Der Blaue Reiter" (The Blue Rider). It aimed to show that here were some artists with lots of new ideas—galloping along on a new form of art.

This new art movement was called Expressionism*—from the word "express," to show or communicate something. In works by the Expressionist painters, the colors and shapes of objects are not natural but have been changed so as to say something specific.

**Further reading**
*The Blue Rider: The Yellow Cow Sees the World in Blue* by Doris Kutschbach (in Prestel's Adventures in Art series)

**What color would you choose for your favorite animal?**

**Paolo as Harlequin, 1924**
Musée Picasso, Paris

Paolo's mother was Picasso's first wife, the Russian ballet dancer Olga Khokhlova. Paolo's harlequin costume recalls Picasso's other paintings of circus artists. What sort of costume would you wear if you had your portrait painted?

1936 Spanish Civil War ✱ 1937 The town of Guernica is bombed
1937 World Fair in Paris: Picasso paints Guernica

✱ 1940–1944 German troops occupy Paris
1939–1945 Second World War

st World War

1920     1925     1930     1935     1940     1945     1950     1955     1960     1965     1970     1975

# Pablo Picasso—The Artistic Genius

Pablo Picasso is the most famous artists of the twentieth century. His inventiveness and the number of works he created are legendary. In his art he was continually searching for new ways of looking at the world.

Picasso could do everything: Draw, paint, and produce sculptures. At the age of eleven he started to attend art school. Two years later he could already paint better than his father, who was also an artist as well as being an art teacher. Legend has it that he decided to stop painting and gave his son his palette, brushes, and paints.

But Picasso was not satisfied with merely copying objects and people. He wanted to discover something new. Children, he thought, always have surprisingly new ideas. And so he practiced for years until he could paint like a child once again. He wanted to see the world with the eyes of a child, and to be as curious and open-minded as they are.

**Born:**
   October 25, 1881 in
   Málaga, Spain
**Died:**
   April 8, 1973 in
   Mougins, France
**Lived in:**
   Spain and France
**Painting styles:**
   Many different ones;
   he kept on trying out
   new things
**Children:**
   Paolo, Maya, Claude,
   Paloma
**Hobby:**
   Bullfighting

**The Saltimbanque, 1905**
National Gallery of Art,
Washington, D.C.

Saltimbanques were street artists, clowns, harlequins, and actors who went from one town to the next to present their show. They were usually poor and had no real home as they were always on the move. They had no other choice if they wanted to be performers. Picasso, the artist, compares himself with them.

**Tip**
Under www.picasso.fr
you will find a website with
funny drawings and other
bits of interesting information—all in English too.

Picasso moved to Paris when he was 23 because the capital of France
was also the capital of the art world in those days. Nonetheless he
remained a true Spaniard with all his heart and soul for the rest of his
life.

Picasso belonged to a group of painters and writers who rejected
middle-class life with all its fixed rules. Like the traveling performers in
Picasso's pictures they wanted to be outsiders, and more than anything
else, they wanted to be free. Even their art was totally different.

**Guernica, 1937**
Museo Nacional Centro de Arte Reina Sofia, Madrid

Civil war broke out in Spain in 1937. In the same year, Picasso painted the picture *Guernica* for the Spanish Pavilion at the World Fair in Paris. Shortly before, German aircraft had bombed the little town of Guernica in northern Spain. The picture is a condemnation of war in general. The world has descended into chaos. The disintegrated forms show the pain and destruction of war. There are no bright colors, just black, white, and gray.

**Further reading**
*A Day with Picasso* by Susanne Pfleger (in Prestel's Adventures in Art series); *living_art: Pablo Picasso* by Hajo Düchting

Picasso never stopped working. During the course of his long life he didn't discover just one new painting style—he invented several, which he then mixed with each other. The most important was Cubism*, which amazed people at the beginning of the twentieth century. In his painting *Guernica* Picasso returned to the language of Cubism.

Because of his inventiveness and tireless creative energy, many people think of Picasso as the greatest artistic genius of the twentieth century.

1917 Russian Revolution ✳    ✳ 1922 The Soviet Union is founded

Marc Chagall 1887–1985

Franz Marc 1880–1916                                                1917–1921 Civil War in Russia

Pablo Picasso 1881–1973

1914–1918 First World War

1880    1885    1890    1895    1900    1905    1910    1915    1920    1925    1930    1935

**Born:**
July 7, 1887 in
Vitebsk, Belarus

**Died:**
March 28, 1985 in
Saint-Paul-de-Vence,
France

**Lived in:**
Vitebsk, St. Peters-
burg, Moscow, Paris,
New York, High Falls
(N.Y.), Vence, Saint-
Paul-de-Vence

**Painting style:**
Expressionism*,
Surrealism*

**Children:**
Ida, David

# Marc Chagall— Pictures which Tell Stories

Marc Chagall originally wanted to become a dancer—then a singer, then a poet. In the end he became a painter who tells stories like poems in his pictures.

They are stories which Chagall cannot explain in words, but which he can only express in pictures. He paints houses, people, and animals which hover above the surface of the picture. Memories from the past overlap with pictures from the present, as in a dream. The boundaries between time and place have been removed.

Chagall grew up as the son of deeply religious Jews in a suburb of the town of Vitebsk in Belarus. When he was 23 he went to Paris. There he came into contact with the most progressive art of the times. He was enchanted by the luminous colors of Matisse and the Fauves, and he loved the geometric shapes of Picasso and the other Cubists*, which look like crystals.

"Paris! For me it was the loveliest word in the world," said Chagall, although he also loved his native land as well. He often thought of it and in his pictures we can often see his memories of his childhood in Russia.

Paint the town or village where you live and include all the details which you especially love and find important!

## I and the Village, 1911
Museum of Modern Art, New York

Chagall's parents kept a white cow with "milk as white as snow; the cow which talked to us," remembered Chagall. Here in the picture she doesn't just look like an ordinary cow being milked: She also appears very large along with the artist himself. She looks at him gently, in a friendly manner, like a close friend. It looks as if Chagall is offering her a blossoming twig. What else can you see in the picture?

### Tip
Chagall's works can be found in many major museums in Europe, America, Japan, and Israel. You can also see his stained-glass windows for example in the UN Building in New York.

### Further reading
*Marc Chagall: Life is a Dream* by Britta Höpler (in Prestel's Adventures in Art series)

Frida Kahlo 1907–1954 ✳ 1925 Frida is badly injured in an accident

Diego Rivera 1886–1957
Pablo Picasso 1881–1973
Marc Chagall 1887–1985

1914–1918 First World War

1939–1945 Second World W

1890    1895    1900    1905    1910    1915    1920    1925    1930    1935    1940    194

**Born:**
July 6, 1907 in
Coyoacán, a suburb of
Mexico City

**Died:**
July 13, 1954 in
Coyoacán

**Lived in:**
Coyoacán and in the
USA from 1930 to
1933

**Painting style:**
Surrealism*

**Children:**
Frida Kahlo would
have loved to have
had children, but she
was unable to have
any

**My Grandparents,
My Parents, and I, 1936**
Museum of Modern Art, New
York

In this picture, Frida Kahlo
painted herself as a little girl.
She is standing in the garden
of her parents' house. In the
picture above her head you
can see her parents in their
wedding finery. Little Frida
is already in her mother's
stomach. In the clouds on the
left and right-hand side of
the picture Frida has painted
her grandparents. Her family
tree is surrounded by the
Mexican landscape.

# Frida Kahlo—
# The Story of a Life in Pictures

Frida Kahlo tells us a great deal about herself and
her life in her paintings.

It wasn't easy: When she was a child, Frida Kahlo suffered from polio, and
then, when she was 18, she broke her spine in a traffic accident. She had
to spend many months in hospital. In order to fill in the hours of bore-
dom, she started to paint. Painting finally became her profession. She
never really recovered from the accident. She had to have lots of opera-
tions and she was constantly in pain. She portrayed the events in her life,
her experiences, and her longings in her pictures.

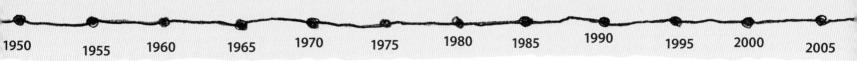

**Self-Portrait as a Tehuana, 1943**
Private collection

Frida Kahlo loved her country very much. She often wore Mexican costume and jewelry. Here she has painted herself wearing the costume of a Mexican Indian woman belonging to the Tehuana people. The women were confident and proud, just like Frida herself. On her forehead you can see the picture of a man. It is the artist Diego Rivera, whom Frida married when she was 23 years old. Why do you think she has painted him like that?

**Tips**
Today, Frida Kahlo's Blue House in Mexico City has been turned into the Frida Kahlo Museum. You can find more information about her in English under http://fkahlo.com.

**Further reading**
*Frida Kahlo: The Artist in the Blue House* by Magdalena Holzhey (in Prestel's Adventures in Art series)

Why not draw your own family tree with your parents and grandparents? Perhaps you can add your brothers and sisters as well!

1941 USA enters the Second World War ✳
Andy Warhol 1928–1987

✳ 1945 USA drop atomic
bombs on Hiroshima and
Nagasaki in Japan

Pablo Picasso 1881–1973

Marc Chagall 1887–1985

1939–1945 Second World War

1900    1905    1910    1915    1920    1925    1930    1935    1940    1945    1950    195

**Early Liz (Colored Liz),
1963**
Private Collection

During the 1960s
Elizabeth Taylor was con-
sidered to be one of the
most beautiful women in
the world. Andy Warhol
created a whole series
of pictures of her. That
is why you can see the
pictures of the film star
in lots of different bright
and cheerful colors.

# Andy Warhol—Superstar

"Everything is beautiful," is what Andy Warhol used to say, and lived his life along these lines.

Whether it was a can of tomato soup from the supermarket; the actress Marilyn Monroe; or copies of famous works from the history of art—they all appear in his pictures. Anything as long as it is large and brightly colored. Warhol didn't make any difference between everyday objects and great works of art.

**Born:**
August 6, 1928 as Andy Warhola in Pittsburgh, Pennsylvania, USA
**Died:**
February 22, 1987 in New York
**Painting style:**
Pop Art*

And his pictures didn't have to be painted as one-off works of art either. Andy Warhol liked using silkscreen and offset printing which were normally used for running off advertising posters. He had learned all about techniques like these when he was studying art and design, and then during the time he worked as a graphic artist in an advertising agency. By using silkscreen printing it was possible to make lots of copies of a picture—like in a factory.

Warhol then gave up his studio and set up an art workshop instead which he called "The Factory," where he could produce pictures like industrial products with the help of a large staff of assistants. It was here, too, that Warhol made films and took photographs—or released strangely shaped clouds that rose up into the sky from the roof of the factory: balloons which he had had made of silver foil.

**Campbell's Tomato Soup, 1968**
Private Collection

There had never been anything like it before: an enormous soup can, right in the middle of the picture, as if it were something very valuable, for no real reason! Warhol loved the consumer world. Later he also painted detergent packets or piled them up like a sculpture.

41

Andy Warhol didn't think that he was very good looking, and when was only 25, he bought himself a hairpiece. He had his nose re-shaped by a cosmetic surgeon. He liked to wear dark sunglasses instead of his horn-rimmed spectacles. It didn't make him look exactly handsome, but at least he looked interesting.

**Flowers, 1964**
Private Collection

Warhol used a photo of hibiscus flowers from a magazine as the basis for these flowers. There are about 900 pictures of flowers like this, in lots of bright colors. Sometimes Warhol finished as many as 80 of them in a single day with a little help from his friends.

You could find Andy Warhol everywhere in New York where something important was happening. His dazzling personality and unusual appearance made him a sort of superstar. Everybody who thought he was anybody wanted to have his portrait done by Warhol. And so Andy Warhol became the most famous artist of the Pop Art* movement.

**Do It Yourself: Violin, 1962**
Private collection

In shops selling art supplies, amateur artists could buy paintboxes with painting templates where the shapes are already marked out. With "painting by numbers" you only have to paint the marked areas the right color. Serious artists would never use a template of that kind. For Warhol, however, the boundary between kitsch and great art no longer existed.

**Further reading**
*Andy Warhol: Paintings for Children* by Silvia Neysters and Sabine Söll-Tauchert; and *Pop Art* by Christian Demilly (both in Prestel's Adventures in Art series)

# Glossary

**ACADEMY OF ART**   A college where students can study art (painting, drawing, sculpture, plus—nowadays— photography and film making).

**ANATOMY**   The structure of the body. Anatomy also refers to the branch of medicine which looks into the form and structure of the body and its organs.

**BAROQUE**   The word "Baroque" comes from the Portuguese *barocco*, describing an irregularly shaped pearl which is not a true sphere. During the Baroque period architecture had a preference for arched forms which were full of movement. In those times many painters began to be especially interested in portraying everyday life. Others depicted dramatic scenes from the Bible or mythology. Carefully planned color schemes and impressive effects of light and shade fascinated the artists of the time. The Baroque age lasted from about 1600 until the mid-18th century.

**BAUHAUS**   A famous German college for art, design, and architecture. It was founded in Weimar, Germany, in 1919 and moved to Dessau in 1925. From 1932 until it was closed by the National Socialists (Nazis) the Bauhaus was located in Berlin. The Bauhaus developed completely new ideas about what houses, furniture, and everyday objects should look like. They should be simple, attractive, and practical and not too expensive. The influence of the Bauhaus on architects and designers can still be felt today. Paul Klee and other painters taught the students of the Bauhaus the basic rules of artistic design.

**COMPLEMENTARY COLORS**   Theoretically speaking, complementary colors produce black when they are mixed together. In practice, however, this does not work because paints do not just contain pure color; they also contain binders and fillers. Complementary pairs of colors contain all three primary colors (red, blue, and yellow): red – green (blue + yellow), blue – orange (red + yellow), yellow – purple (red + blue): If the complementary colors are put next to each other, each makes the other look even more brilliant.

**CUBISM**   The word comes from the Latin word *cubus*, meaning a square or cube. Objects and figures are dissected into geometric forms and are shown simultaneously from several different angles—from the front, from the back, from the top. Cubism was developed in around 1908 by Pablo Picasso and his artist friend Georges Braque—who then provoked an artistic revolution.

**EXPRESSIONISM**   The name was invented in 1911. Expressionist painting does not portray the external appearance of objects. Instead, it aims to bring out their true being or the painter's own view. That is why Expressionist painters changed the forms of things and used intensive colors. The painters of "Die Brücke" group of artists, formed in 1905, were important representatives of Expressionism, as were the members of the "Blauer Reiter" (The Blue Rider) group, which was established in 1911. Both groups were founded in Germany.

**FAUVISM**   The Fauves artists used such bright colors for their paintings that the public of the time was horrified. In 1905 the critics attacked the artists calling them *fauves*—wild animals, so the group decided to use the name. The head of the group was Henri Matisse. The group was dissolved only two years later, but it provided the Expressionists with important new ideas.

**IMPRESSIONISM**   A style of painting which arose in France between 1860 and 1870 and which had a strong influence on painting in both Europe and America. The name refers to the painting *Impression* by Claude Monet. The Impressionists aimed to show the visual impression the scene made on them by means of shimmering dots of light and color. The Impressionists especially liked working outdoors because it is outside that the light conditions and colors change most noticeably depending on the time of day and the season. Late Impressionism began in about 1880, when painters like Vincent van Gogh and Paul Gauguin became less and less interested in painting the world as it really is.

**LATE IMPRESSIONISM**   see Impressionism

**NUDE DRAWING** Drawing from a live model in order to look at the shape and movement of the human body. Nude drawing used to be one of the traditional subjects studied by artists or sculptors during their training.

**PIGMENT** The Latin word *pigmentum* means "dye." Pigments are small particles, as fine as dust, which give paints their color. To make paint they are mixed with a binder, for example with oil for oil paints. In former times, pigments were made from soil, rock or from plant or animal substances (for example, purplish red came from the purple murex, a type of snail; indigo comes from woad). The most precious color of all was the blue from the semi-precious stone lapis lazuli. It is called "ultramarine" because the stone came from countries beyond the sea (Latin: *ultra mare*). The pigment is more expensive than gold, which is why today ultramarine—like many other pigments—is manufactured artificially.

**POP ART** "Pop" comes from "popular," which means easily understood, well-loved. The art style, which developed at the end of the 1950s and which determined what happened in art during the 1960s, was so named because it worked with pictures, objects, and methods based on everyday life.

You can make colors to paint with. You can buy pigments in stores selling artists' materials. Mix some wallpaper paste according to the instructions on the packet and stir in the pigments thoroughly as required—and there you have your paints! If you haven't got any pigments you can cook elderberries, red hollyhock flowers, red cabbage, and onions and use the liquid as a dye.

**RENAISSANCE** The word comes from the French and means "rebirth." In the Renaissance era, which extended from the first half of the 15th century to about 1600, the art of Ancient Rome and Greece was rediscovered—an era during which people had already shown a great interest in the way things looked.

**RESTORATION** To repair a damaged artwork or building.

**SURREALISM** Surrealism is interested in what goes beyond reality—*sur* in French means "on" or "above." The expression was used for the first time in 1917, and during the 1920s and 1930s the Surrealists—writers and sculptors as well as artists—attracted a lot of attention. Familiar things were presented in way never seen before and were linked to surprising and mysterious paintings in a dreamlike manner. For the Surrealists the wonderful,

mysterious, and unreal was just as real as everyday reality.

**WATERCOLOR** Water-soluble paints which can be painted over with water and which contain a large proportion of fine pigments with gum Arabic used as a binder. Watercolors are not opaque; they permit the background—mostly a special type of white paper—to shine through, making the colors translucent.

**WORLD FAIR** International exhibitions at which the participating countries presented themselves and their achievements in technology, industry, and the arts and crafts.

## Answers to the quiz:

Page 9:         Precious ultramarine blue is made from lapis lazuli (see glossary).

Page 18:        Van Gogh probably painted his self-portrait in front of a mirror; that is why
                you see him the wrong way round.

Page 31:        The group of artists surrounding Franz Marc and Wassily Kandinsky is
                known as "Der Blaue Reiter" (The Blue Rider).

Library of Congress Control Number: 2008943396; British Library Cataloguing-in-Publication Data: a catalogue record for this book is available from the British Library; Deutsche Nationalbibliothek holds a record of this publication in the Deutsche Nationalbibliografie; detailed bibliographical data can be found under: http://dnb.ddb.de

© Prestel Verlag, Munich · London · New York 2009.
7th printing  2014

© for the illustrated works by Marc Chagall: VG Bild-Kunst, Bonn, 2014; Frida Kahlo: Banco de México Diego Rivera & Frida Kahlo Museums Trust / VG Bild-Kunst, Bonn 2014; Henri Matisse: Succession H. Matisse / VG Bild-Kunst, Bonn 2014; Pablo Picasso: Succession Picasso / VG Bild-Kunst Bonn 2014; Andy Warhol: Andy Warhol Foundation for the Visual Arts / Artists Rights Society, New York 2014

Credits for pictures by Paul Klee: *Hammamet*, 1914,48, watercolor and pencil on paper on card, 20.3 x 15.7 cm, Öffentliche Kunstsammlung Basel, Kupferstichkabinett; *The Twittering Machine*, 1922.151, oil tracing and watercolor on paper, worked with watercolor and pen, on card, 41.3 x 30.5 cm, The Museum of Modern Art, New York; *Landscape with Yellow Birds*, 1923.32, watercolor and chalk on black foundation on paper, cut and re-combined, finished with gouache and pen, on card, 35.5 x 44 cm, private collection, Switzerland; *Ad Parnassum*, 1932.274 (x14), oil paints, lines stamped, dots initially stamped in white and subsequently painted over, on canvas with stretcher frame, colored wooden frame, 100 x 125 cm, Kunstmuseum Bern.

Picture credits: Unless otherwise indicated, pictorial material has been taken from the Publisher's archives; Artothek pp. 21, 25, 28–31, 34/35; Rafael Doniz p. 39; Zentrum Paul Klee p. 27.

Front cover: Details taken from works by Vermeer (p. 9), Marc (p. 30), Klee (p. 26)
Frontispiece: Vincent van Gogh, *Portrait as an Artist*, 1888, Van Gogh Museum, Amsterdam

Prestel books are available worldwide. Please contact your nearest bookseller or one of the following addresses for information concerning your local distributor.

Prestel, a member of
Verlagsgruppe Random House GmbH

www.prestel.de

Prestel Publishing Ltd.
14-17 Wells Street
London W1T 3PD

Prestel Publishing
900 Broadway, Suite 603, New York, NY 10003
www.prestel.com

Translation: Jane Michael, Munich
Copyediting: Christopher Wynne, Bad Tölz

Project management and editing: Doris Kutschbach
Design: Michael Schmölzl, agenten.und.freunde, Munich
Production: Astrid Wedemeyer
Origination: Reproline mediateam, Munich
Printing and Binding: Printer Trento, Trento

Verlagsgruppe Random House FSC® N001967
The FSC®-certified paper *Hello Fat Matt* has been produced by mill Condat, Le Lardin Saint-Lazare, France.

ISBN 978-3-7913-4173-6